THE PLOT DOT

A Visual Guide to Plotting Your Novel

and creating unforgettable scenes

DEREK MURPHY

Copyright @ Derek Murphy, 2016

www.creativindie.com

When I started writing fiction, I was surprised to discover the techniques I'd learned designing over a thousand book covers came in handy. I still needed to learn stuff like plotting, story architecture and character development, but there was one thing I seemed to be really good at: painting pictures in readers' minds.

My art and design background made me really good at visualizing scenes. I even developed some mental tricks for creating powerful, resonant scenes that stick in people's minds, using the same techniques that make my book covers stand out and get noticed.

I started thinking of each scene as one perfect picture.

This book will help you paint powerful visual scenes that stick with readers long after they're finished reading. The technique I describe is simple and easy to use. I combined it with blank pages and a guided space to help you plot your book visually.

There are lots of systems and guides to plotting, but if you're like me you have journals filled with notes, and it can get overwhelming. This book will help you get organized and unlock hidden potential in your scenes that you didn't know was there, by going *beyond words* and focusing on *drawing and coloring* your scenes, one by one, until you have a full outline.

I won't focus on each and every scene (though I will leave blank pages so you can fill them in). But I will focus on the major scenes that most stories will include, based on my understanding of a classic 3-Act structure and Joseph Campbell's *Hero's Journey.*

HOW TO USE THIS BOOK

Let me introduce you to some of the techniques I use in cover design; these are the same basics I'll ask you to use when you visualize your scenes.

1. Lots of light and dark contrast
2. Lots of color contrast
3. A humanizing element
4. A dash of color to focus your eye
5. Something that symbolizes the conflict in the scene

You might already have your scenes in mind – you have the setting. You may have described the characters and the action, it might be good. But it doesn't stick visually. That's what setting and description is for. In every scene, you need to plant a red flag, what I'm calling a "plot dot." It's a bright bit of color that draws the eye. It helps readers focus on what's interesting and important about the scene. It doesn't *have* to be red, but it should be described in detail. If it's a black or white feather, the color of the feather will be described in such detail readers can't stop thinking about it.

Usually when you write scenes, you map out what happens. Here we are ONLY going to draw it, though you can make notes. Keep in mind it's OK to shift scenes around later, if you need to – you can rip the pages out of this book to rearrange them, though I don't think that's necessary; you can just refer back to the right drawing for each scene while writing, even if they're out of order. That's one of the benefits of visualizing scenes like this; each scene should be instantly viewable in its entirety in one powerful image. It makes them unforgettable.

You should sketch these out in pencil at first, and later in pen if you want to. Keep them black and white (though you may want to shade them in), except for the "flash of color."

As an example, think of Nathaniel Hawthorne's *The Scarlet Letter*. He could have just written a book about those characters, in those situations, and it would have been good. But he drew attention to the conflict of all those relationships, and he funneled the righteous judgment of Hester Prynne's peers, along with Hester's own shame and despair, into one bright symbol—*A*—a public badge, a visible reminder, a lens that focuses each scene.

That's what you're looking for. It doesn't have to be as self-conscious or obvious as Hawthorne's, but try to think of something in each scene that deepens the characters or the conflict.

We'll start with your main characters, then go through some major plot events, before giving you space to illustrate each scene in your novel.

Special tip: Use your "flash of color" to make readers *feel* the mood you want them to feel in each scene. Find one object in each scene that's the most colorful, brightest thing in that scene.

PS) Originally I had left room for 100 scene illustrations, on every other page (so you don't have to draw on the back of another illustration). But you probably don't need to illustrate scenes from *every* chapter, and I didn't want the price of this book to be too high because of all the blank pages. So if you need more just use a photocopy machine (it's OK, you have the author's permission).

THE PLOT DOT

USE COLOR TO GIVE READERS *the feels*

ORANGE
Joy, Creativity, Optimism, Freedom, Warmth, Adventure, Daring, Independence, Curiosity, Rigidity, Persistence, Impatience

YELLOW
Fun, Celebration, Humor, Happiness, Intellect, Sarcasm, Confidence, Competition, Celebration, Selfishness, Distracted, Busy, Stubborness

RED
Love, Death, Passion, Anger, Vitality, Power, Intensity, Hunger, Determination, Resentment, Anxiety

GREEN
Freshness, Harmony, Friendship, Empathy, Prosperity, Nature, Jealousy, Altruism, Communication

PINK
Luxury, Power, Mystery, Royalty, Domineering, Greedy, Spiritual Crisis, Overwhelmed, Emotional

TURQUOISE
Safety, Foundation, Hope, Education, Healing, Loyalty, Compassion, Sophistication, Idealism

PURPLE
Quiet, Intuition, Denial, Imagination, Meditation, Intuition, Hallucinations or Nightmares, Obsession

BLUE
Sadness, Distance, Loneliness, Isolation, Longing, Truth, Lies and Secrets, Gossip, Fear, Feeling Stuck

BLACK: Loss, Despair, Tension

WHITE: Purity, Peace, Anxiety

Characters

Protagonist/MC

The main character is the "hero" of the story.

Draw your character. What's interesting about their appearance? How does what they wear express their character? What meaningful object do they carry with them? Where's the flash of color?

Antagonist

The antagonist is the main villain or opposing force.

Draw your character. What's interesting about their appearance? How does what they wear express their character? What meaningful object do they carry with them? Where's the flash of color?

Best Friend(s)/Ally

Often an MC will have two best friends, one boy and one girl.

Draw your character. What's interesting about their appearance? How does what they wear express their character? What meaningful object do they carry with them? Where's the flash of color?

Romantic Interest

Draw your character. What's interesting about their appearance? How does what they wear express their character? What meaningful object do they carry with them? Where's the flash of color?

Mentor

Could be a teacher, parent or guide. Someone older and wiser who teaches them something about their journey.

Draw your character. What's interesting about their appearance? How does what they wear express their character? What meaningful object do they carry with them? Where's the flash of color?

Nemesis

Someone who gets in your MC's way, but isn't actually evil, like a teacher, parent or a police man... though it could also be a bully at school or work.

Draw your character. What's interesting about their appearance? How does what they wear express their character? What meaningful object do they carry with them? Where's the flash of color?

The Gang

Other secondary characters. Add conflict by giving them conflicting personalities: skeptical, emotional, sarcastic, slow and thoughtful, etc.

Draw your characters. What's interesting about their appearance? How does what they wear express their character? What meaningful object do they carry with them? Where's the flash of color?

Non-human roadblocks

Think of the major obstacles or problems your protagonist will face. They might be natural events, forces of nature or twists of fate, accidents or animal attacks—these are major forces that need to be dealt with, but don't have a face. See how many you can draw.

Draw your obstacles like monsters, even if they aren't sentient. What's interesting about their appearance? How does their appearance highlight the threat or danger? How are they meaningfully connected to the protagonist? Where's the flash of color?

Obstacles
Non-human roadblocks

Draw your obstacles like monsters, even if they aren't sentient. What's interesting about their appearance? How does their appearance highlight the threat or danger? How are they meaningfully connected to the protagonist? Where's the flash of color?

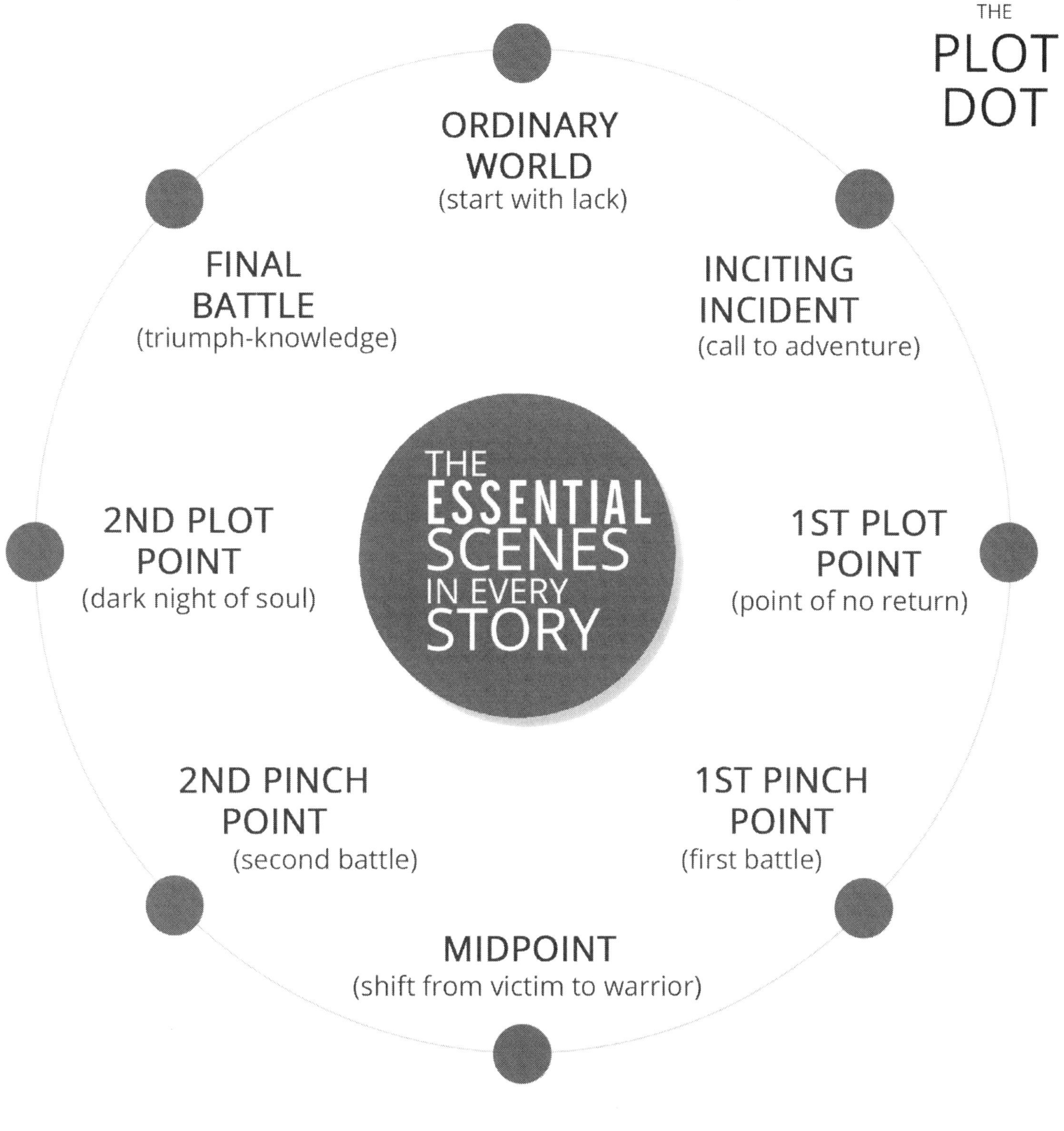

THE PLOT DOT

THE ESSENTIAL SCENES IN EVERY STORY

- **ORDINARY WORLD** (start with lack)
- **INCITING INCIDENT** (call to adventure)
- **1ST PLOT POINT** (point of no return)
- **1ST PINCH POINT** (first battle)
- **MIDPOINT** (shift from victim to warrior)
- **2ND PINCH POINT** (second battle)
- **2ND PLOT POINT** (dark night of soul)
- **FINAL BATTLE** (triumph-knowledge)

Firstly, I should point out that my formula may seem the same as most other 3-Act structures, however it's not identical. After reading dozens of books on plotting, I was still confused. What's the difference between the first plot point and the inciting incident? If they're the same, then nothing at all happen for the first 25% of the book (which is lame). Same thing with the second plot point and final battle—simple plotting graphs lump them together under "climax" but they are very different.

So while this understanding of story was a breakthrough for me, and finally let me map out a successful story, it may be different from what you'll learn about plotting elsewhere. Also, after posting this image online I got a lot of upset writers, who rejected the idea that *every story* is a *hero's journey.* One writer said, "I reject your picture and decide to be creative." Another said, "I need structure? I just want to write."

But the truth is most commercial fiction has a predictable plot structure, and most books that fail to capture readers' imaginations are missing these key plot points. Experienced pantsers can go scene by scene and work their way to the end, but especially if you're working on your first novel, having a little structure can really help you reach the finish line.

Think of structure as training wheels—they'll help you map out the broad strokes, in roughly the right place for maximum emotional impact, based on cues readers have come to expect after consuming thousands of books and movies. This doesn't *stop* you from being creative, though it will probably prevent months of feeling stuck and frustrated.

This is a system that has worked for me personally, and it's based on tons of research, but if it doesn't work for you or it feels constrictive, you're free to try something else. You can use this book even if you don't follow a traditional structure.

We'll start with the eight major plot points—they're the biggest, most powerful scenes in your novel, the bones of the structure. As long as you get these eight points right, your story will have a strong foundation. If you've already plotted your novel, you can just skip what you don't need.

Finally, don't worry about making it pretty. Use stick figures if you have to. This is just a visual reference to help you write faster, better stories. Nobody else has to see it. If you're not comfortable drawing, you can cut out pictures from magazines and make a collage.

Ordinary World
(start with lack)

Your First Act sets up your main character (MC) in their ordinary, mundane environment. You'll introduce their friends and family members, their home, school or workplace, in the first few chapters. But you need to show what's *missing*. You don't want to start with a perfect, happy character who has everything (unless you're going to take it all away, which is fine). You need to give them space to grow. Maybe they have unresolved emotional issues.

They're probably shy, awkward, clumsy or embarrassed, or unpopular. Maybe they hate their job or just got dumped. You need to show what they want, their secret desires. What are they working towards? They probably have daydreams about things they don't think will ever happen.

Draw the ordinary world, surrounding your main character. How is their environment a reflection of their inner flaw? What is their favorite object? Where is the flash of color? Where are the sources of conflict?

Inciting Incident

(call to adventure)

In most books, the inciting incident should actually happen in chapter one or two. It's an *intrusion* on the ordinary world. Something big changes. Maybe a stranger moves to town, or a family member dies, or there's an earthquake. It might be an invitation, or a friend inviting your MC to a party. It can't be a *huge* crisis, but it will be annoying and noticeable, or exciting—it's the beginning of your plot.

That's why you want to get the ball rolling pretty early, otherwise nothing will be happening. Avoid writing a lot of history of backstory. Start your book as near to the inciting incident as you can. But don't think of it as just one scene or chapter.

The "call to adventure" is usually followed by denial or refusal. The MC doesn't trust it, or doesn't want to make a decision. They'll ignore it and continue focusing on their previous goals. They just want things to go back to normal.

Draw the Inciting Incident. What object symbolizes the event and deepens character? How does the setting reflect the mood of the conflict? What's remarkable and novel about the character and their setting? Where is the flash of color?

1st Plot Point
(point of no return)

Things have been getting weirder and/or more intriguing for several chapters. Your MC tries to ignore the problems but they keep interfering with their normal agenda. They get roped in, and something happens that forces them into the action. Everything changes, and there's no going back to the ordinary world. They might have met a teacher, or they might have seen something that changes their perspective: a revelation of supernatural abilities; a murder or death; an accident or robbery or attack or disaster. Something pretty big, that shatters what they thought they understood of the world, and makes them feel vulnerable and exposed. This will be one of the major scenes in your book, so make it unforgettable.

Also, this is the end of Act One, about 25% of your book—by now all the major characters should have already been introduced, or at least hinted at.

Draw the 1st Plot Point. This is your protagonist stepping off the cliff, or going into the rabbit hole. It may not be a physical change of location. What object symbolizes this transition? How does the environment reflect the inner change? What flash of color conveys the mood?

1st Pinch Point

(first battle)

After the 1st Plot Point, there will be several chapters where the protagonist is learning about the new world. They might be doing research, or discovering things in conversations. There needs to be conflict and tension, which builds up to the 1st Pinch Point.

This doesn't have to be a literal battle, but it is the first major interaction with the antagonist. The antagonist might not be visible yet, but he/she should be the one wielding the strings. The antagonist is *after* something, and that something is tied to the MC somehow. Maybe the AC wants something the MC has, or needs the MC to do something, or has a score to settle. The MC probably still has no idea what's happening, but they find themselves at the center of some conflict.

They probably don't *win,* but they do survive. Now the stakes are clear. You should make them as dire as possible, almost inconceivable. Ask yourself, what's the worst thing that could happen? Then ask, how can I make it *even worse* for my protagonist? The stakes should always seem life and death to the protagonist... they represent a complete change, the "death" of the former self, which is why the antagonist resists them. If your protagonist doesn't have their self-identity shaken to its roots, you need to make this scene bigger.

Draw the 1ˢᵗ Pinch Point. This is the first major interaction with the antagonist or the forces of evil. It demonstrates what's at stake. What can you add to make the setting reflect the mood? What can you add to make it epic? What can you add to deepen character? Where is the flash of color? What's remarkable about the setting?

Midpoint
(shift from victim to warrior)

After the 1st Pinch Point, the protagonist continues to face new challenges, but they are in a defensive role. They might be making some plans, but mostly they're waiting for something to happen and reacting to events or circumstances beyond their control. If they try to solve any issue, they end up being thwarted or making things even worse.

They might accidentally hurt someone, or their friends and family begin to fear and distrust them (because they have secrets now). They begin questioning their identity and world view, which leads to a personality crisis, which leads to a shift in perspective. This is about half way through the novel, and marks the point where the protagonist *decides* to take action. They decide to stop being a victim and reacting to events, and vow to do whatever it takes to win. They'll probably form a new goal, and even if they aren't sure how to achieve it yet, they'll feel a deep conviction towards it. This might be based in rage or anger towards the antagonist, a newfound perspective or increased self-confidence.

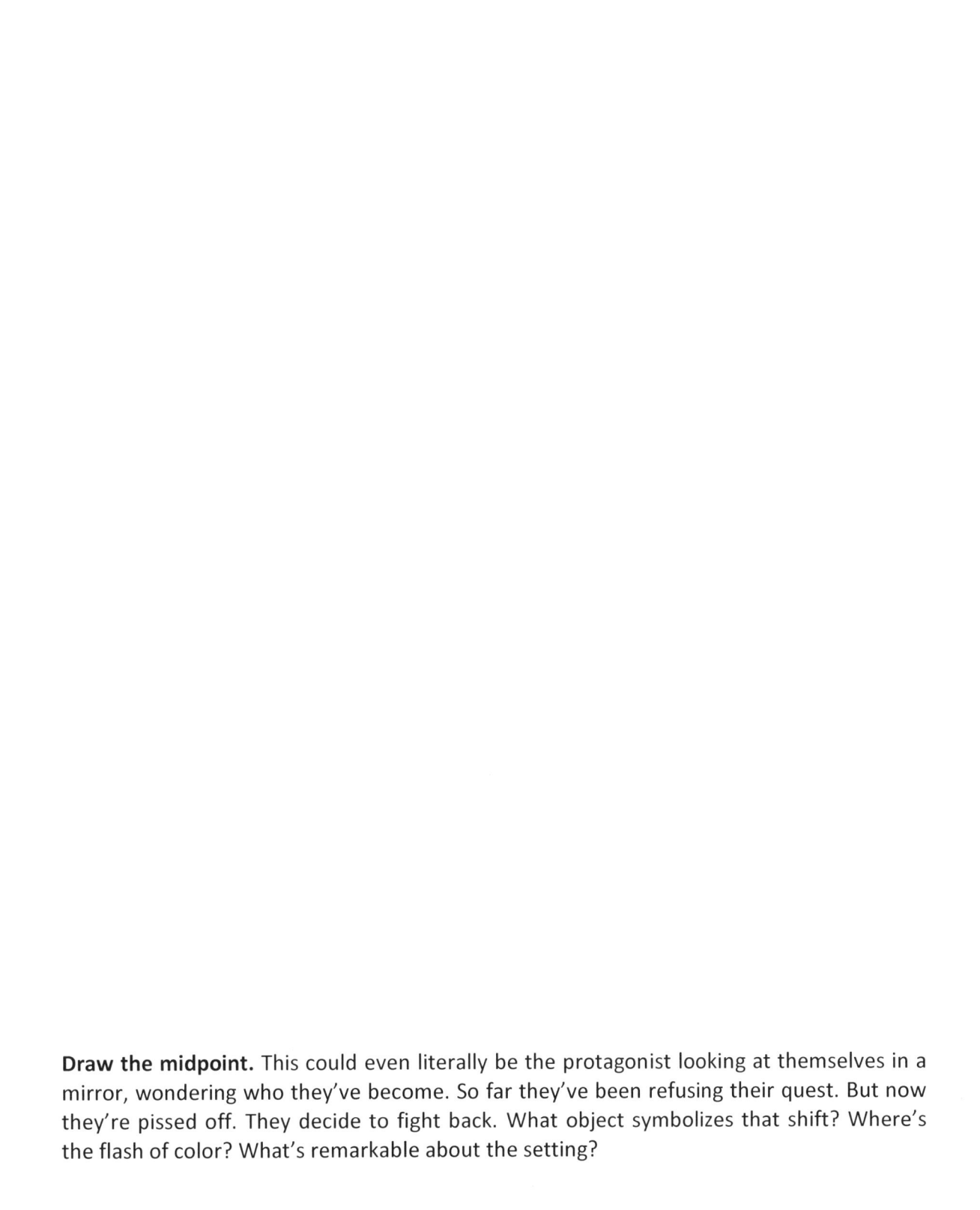

Draw the midpoint. This could even literally be the protagonist looking at themselves in a mirror, wondering who they've become. So far they've been refusing their quest. But now they're pissed off. They decide to fight back. What object symbolizes that shift? Where's the flash of color? What's remarkable about the setting?

2ⁿᵈ Pinch Point

(second battle)

This leads to a second confrontation with the antagonist. It still may not be the main villain; it could just be henchmen that represent the main villain's interests. It could be an attack, or it could be the result of the MC taking action, such as setting a trap for the AC (or vice-versa, the villain can set a trap for the MC, for example by kidnapping a friend or relative).

The protagonist is determined to see this through, and feels personally responsible, even though the chances of success are slim.

The conflict erupts into an open battle, with escalating consequences; or it could just be something really bad that happens, as a result of the antagonist's actions.

This confrontation makes the protagonist realize that everything is *much worse* than they thought, and they realize they've underestimated the antagonist's power. They rally with new determination, and might even score a seeming victory.

Draw the 2nd Pinch Point. In this scene, the antagonist defeats the protagonist's forces, or foreshadows what's at stake in the next major encounter. What object symbolizes the danger and conflict? Where's the flash of color? What is remarkable about the setting?

2nd Plot Point

(dark night of the soul)

The plan failed. The secret weapon backfired. The hero's team was slaughtered, or they lost their one advantage, or the AC's evil plan succeeded. The worst has happened. The antagonist has won.

Alternatively, the 2nd Pinch Point can be elevated conflict, followed by MC reaction. Maybe the antagonist has stolen something or kidnapped an ally. They rally the troops, and try fix things, but things keep getting worse and worse, leading to a total, devastating loss. Usually this process happens over several chapters. But at the 2nd Plot Point, everything the MC feared could happen, has happened. They are destroyed. They cannot win. They give up. There's no hope.

They lose the battle, with serious consequences. Someone the protagonist cares about got hurt, and they feel guilty. Usually the failure is due to their character flaw or a lack of knowledge.

This marks a period of depression, prompting a change in mindset—the AC has to *give up* what they want. They realize that the thing they've been holding on to (often it's just wanting to get back to the ordinary world, back to normal) is completely gone. There is no chance for victory. The only way forward is *through*. They are forced to change and go in a new direction.

This is tied to the MC's flaw/lack of knowledge. When they figure out what they've been holding onto, what's been holding them back or limiting them, and when they're prepared to sacrifice what *they* want, for the greater good, they finally become the hero they need to be to defeat the villain.

Draw the 2nd Plot Point. This is the second major interaction with the antagonist... the protagonist knew this was coming, and thought they were somewhat prepared, but they were wrong. Make this scene heart-wrenching by taking something permanent from them or one of their allies (destroyed house, lost limb, a death...). What object focuses the scene? What object does your MC cling to afterwards, as a reminder?

Final Battle
(triumph-knowledge)

Usually the MC needs a pep talk from a close friend, to "gird the loins." They need a reason to fight, even if it's hopeless. Even if they don't see how to defeat the enemy. There's no choice but to confront them.

But now they are prepared—they might have gained a valuable piece of knowledge or information. They might have been given a new weapon or power, or learned the villain's weakness (or maybe not… they might find that just by going into battle on faith, whatever they need materializes in the critical moment).

The final battle scene often includes a "hero at the mercy of the villain" scene, where the hero is caught, so the villain can gloat (or this can come earlier, just before the 2nd Plot Point). Anyway it's not a clear, easy victory. They *fail* at first, all is lost, the hero is captured, the enemy gloats, *then* the hero perseveres... usually simply by not giving up. With resolve and tenacity, the hero escapes and overpowers the villain. Often the final battle scene also includes a "death of the hero" scene, where the hero, or an ally/romantic interest, sacrifices themselves, and appears to die... but then is brought back to life in joy and celebration. (Or if you want to keep it dark, just have them die, so the victory will be bittersweet).

This doesn't have to be a literal "battle." It's just the last, final straw, the most dramatic part of your story. It's what forces the MC to make a realization, change or grow. And it's the place where the MC has a victory.

Draw the Final Battle. The antagonist if fully revealed. The protagonist rides off to meet their fate. At first they fail, and are captured—all seems lost, but in a sudden twist, the protagonist reaches into themselves and finds the motivation and tenacity to persevere, unlocking access to their secret weapon, and defeating the antagonist. Make it EPIC.

Return to Ordinary

(completion of journey)

The hero returns, changed. They've won, though it's probably temporary (this villain was defeated, but he or someone new will return). The safety is short-lived and bittersweet. The hero once again faces the small challenges or bullies at the beginning of the story, but they seem so trivial now. The hero is no longer lacking; they've grown in confidence, and now have a group of new friends, and a new hope for the future.

Draw the Return to Ordinary. The antagonist has been defeated, but the protagonist is forever changed. What have they lost? What have they gained? What object(s) symbolize those things? Where is the flash of color?

Mapping it out
(Act One)

The First Act will have about 10 to 20 chapters, and take up 25% of the story.

Here are some of the things that often happen in the first act.

- Ordinary world, building empathy
- Inciting event
- An event that creates desire or longing
- Another character asks a question that becomes a theme
- A moral dilemma
- Something embarrassing
- Character realizes external goal
- Attempts to fulfill their longing or need.
- What goal does character take action to reach?
- Call to adventure/refuses quest

- Display of flaw
- Reveals a piece of themselves
- Meets with mentor
- Takes action towards goal
- They can't get what they want, so they change their plan
- Antagonist revealed
- Point of no return, accepts quest and commits to goal
- A problem grows out of character weakness
- New Drive for Goal
- What plan does the antagonist have to reach goal?

Map out your scenes for Act One. List only the location and "what happens."

-
-
-
-
-
-
-
-
-
-

-
-
-
-
-
-
-
-
-
-

Draw a scene. Draw the central conflict or problem. Symbolize it in a centering object. What can you add to make the scene unique? What can you add to make it epic? What can you add to deepen character? Where is the flash of color? Where are the boundaries?

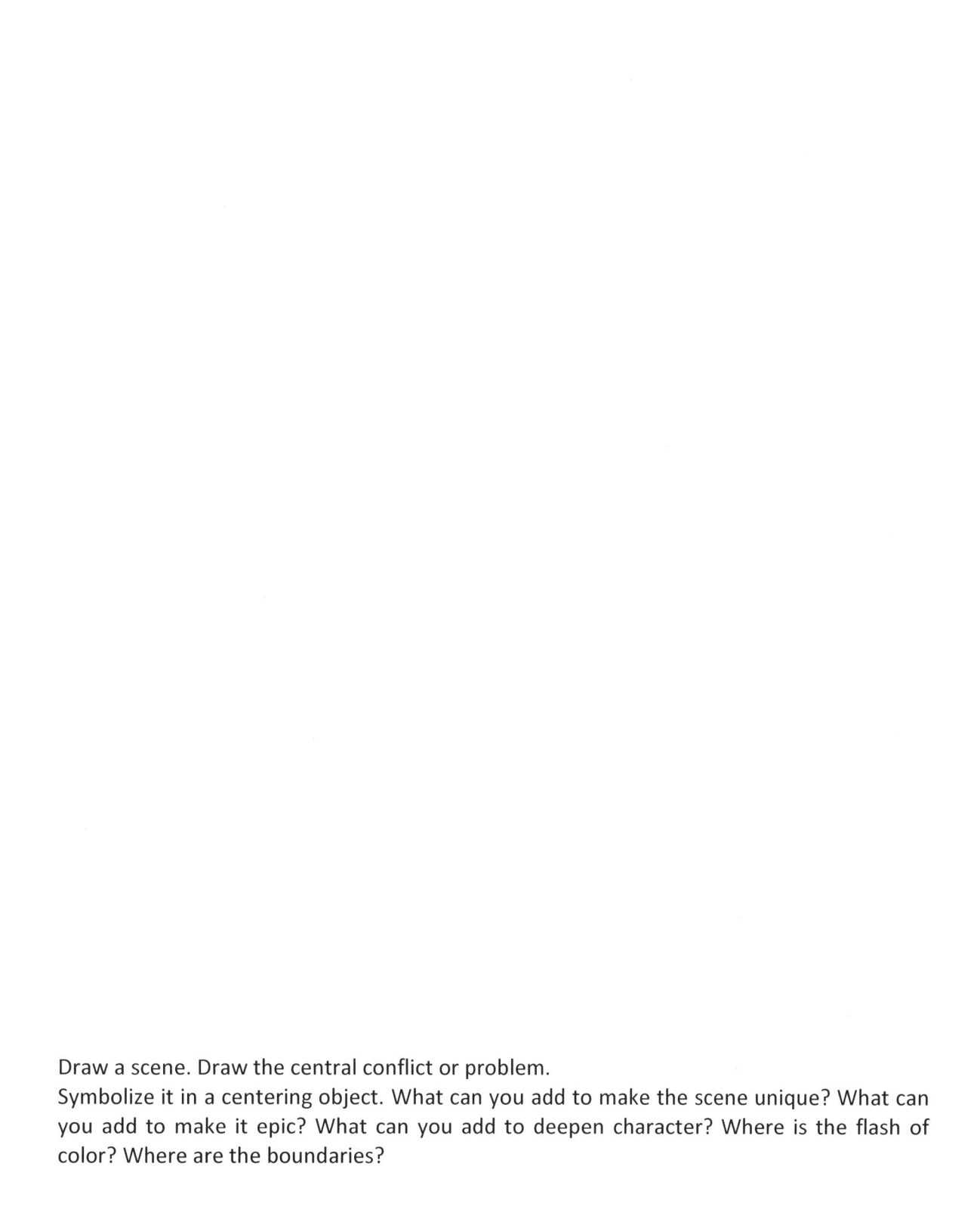

Draw a scene. Draw the central conflict or problem.
Symbolize it in a centering object. What can you add to make the scene unique? What can you add to make it epic? What can you add to deepen character? Where is the flash of color? Where are the boundaries?

Draw a scene. Draw the central conflict or problem. Symbolize it in a centering object. What can you add to make the scene unique? What can you add to make it epic? What can you add to deepen character? Where is the flash of color? Where are the boundaries?

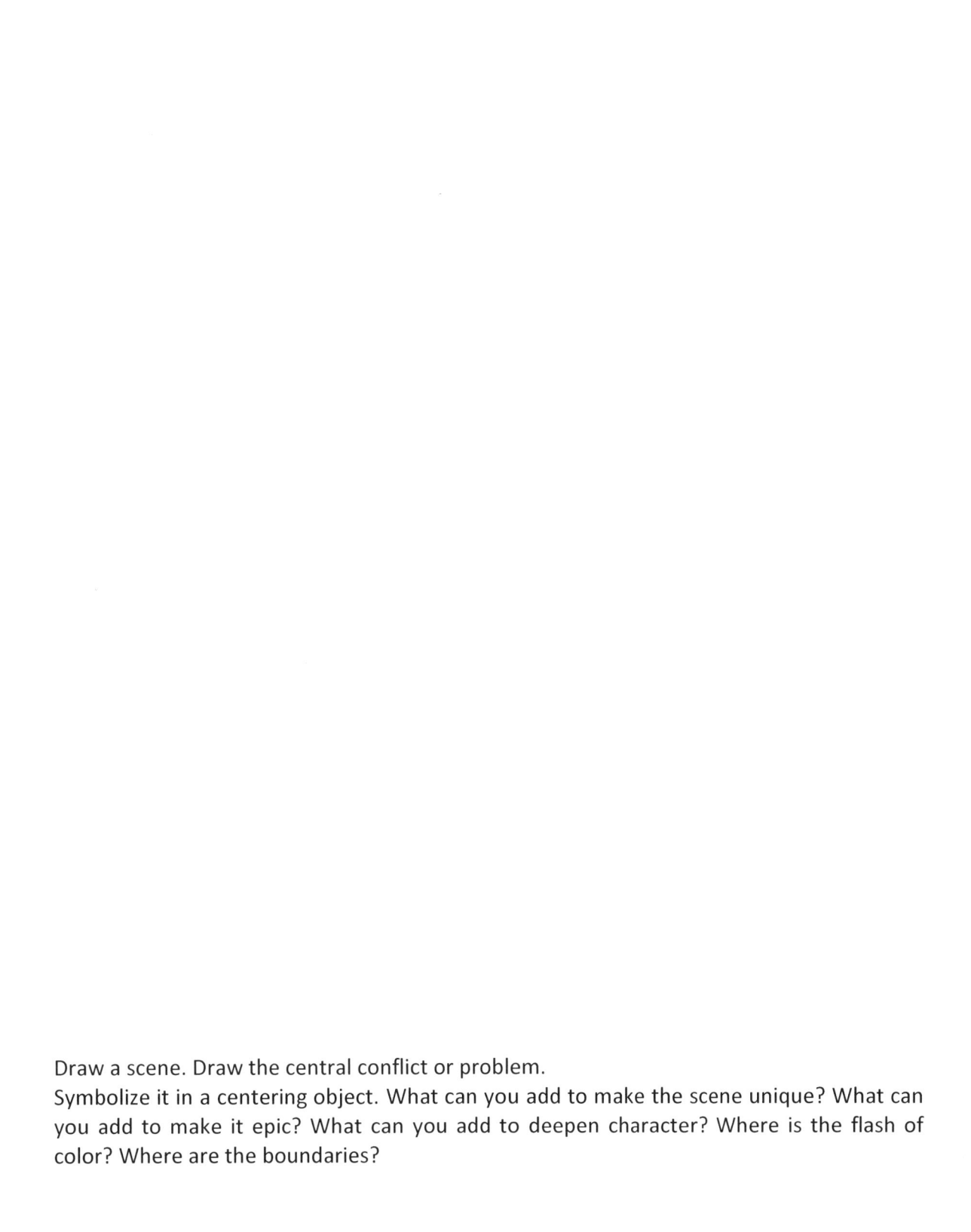

Draw a scene. Draw the central conflict or problem. Symbolize it in a centering object. What can you add to make the scene unique? What can you add to make it epic? What can you add to deepen character? Where is the flash of color? Where are the boundaries?

Draw a scene. Draw the central conflict or problem. Symbolize it in a centering object. What can you add to make the scene unique? What can you add to make it epic? What can you add to deepen character? Where is the flash of color? Where are the boundaries?

Draw a scene. Draw the central conflict or problem. Symbolize it in a centering object. What can you add to make the scene unique? What can you add to make it epic? What can you add to deepen character? Where is the flash of color? Where are the boundaries?

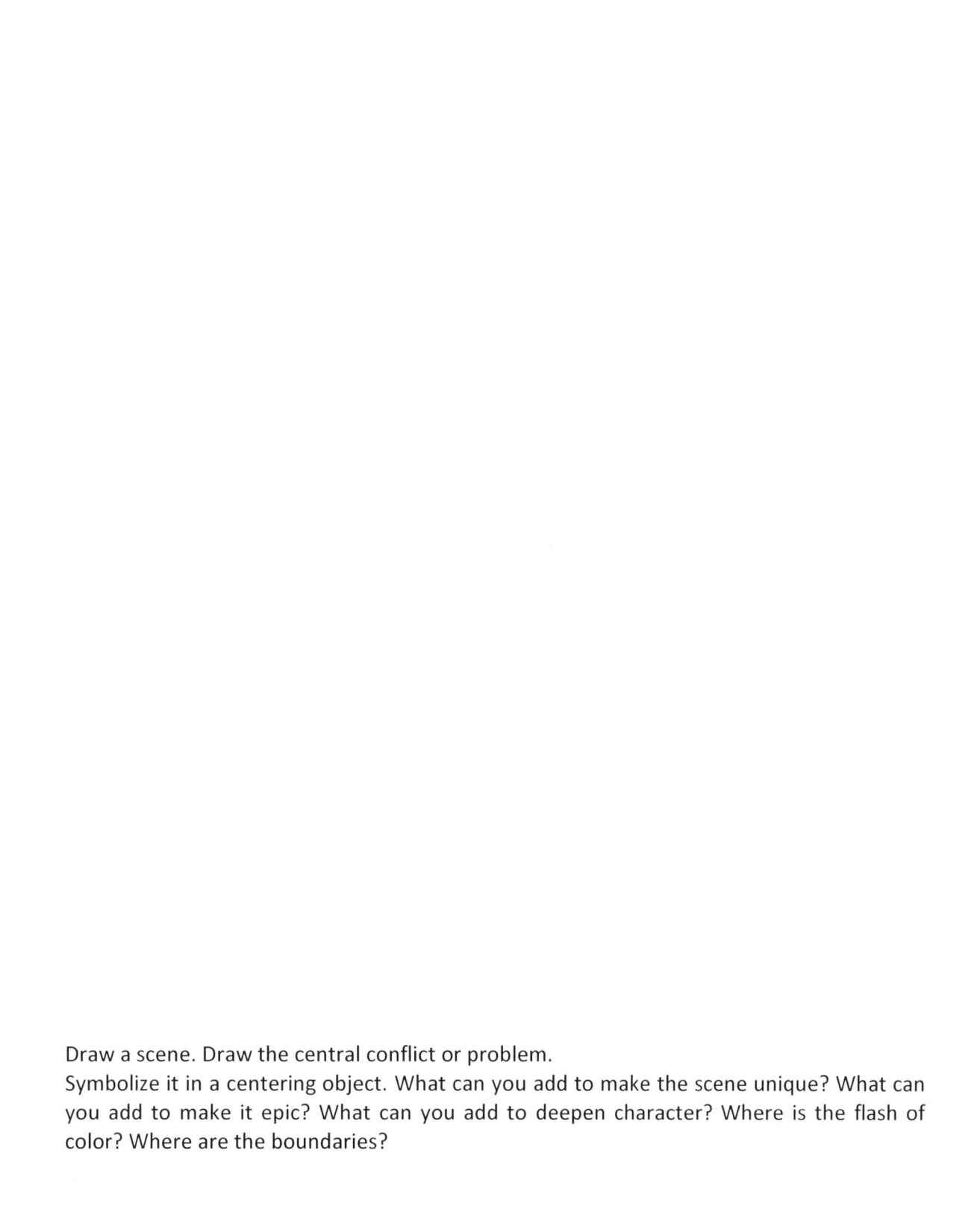

Draw a scene. Draw the central conflict or problem. Symbolize it in a centering object. What can you add to make the scene unique? What can you add to make it epic? What can you add to deepen character? Where is the flash of color? Where are the boundaries?

Draw a scene. Draw the central conflict or problem. Symbolize it in a centering object. What can you add to make the scene unique? What can you add to make it epic? What can you add to deepen character? Where is the flash of color? Where are the boundaries?

Draw a scene. Draw the central conflict or problem. Symbolize it in a centering object. What can you add to make the scene unique? What can you add to make it epic? What can you add to deepen character? Where is the flash of color? Where are the boundaries?

Draw a scene. Draw the central conflict or problem. Symbolize it in a centering object. What can you add to make the scene unique? What can you add to make it epic? What can you add to deepen character? Where is the flash of color? Where are the boundaries?

FIRST PLOT POINT

Draw a scene. Draw the central conflict or problem.
Symbolize it in a centering object. What can you add to make the scene unique? What can you add to make it epic? What can you add to deepen character? Where is the flash of color? Where are the boundaries?

Mapping it out
(Act Two)

The Second Act will have about 20 to 40 chapters, and should take up about 50% of your story. Often the Second Act goes too slowly, because authors are "stalling" until they can get to the exciting final scenes. You'll probably need to fill some chapters with subplots (stories that involve secondary characters). Also, remember to never let your characters get the carrot. Every time they try to do *anything*, throw stuff in their way. They need to go get a pen, then find some paper, so they can leave a note. But the only pen is back at school. And they're out of gas. And there are zombies. So they take bicycles. But then the bicycles break. And the road is blocked. And someone catches on fire. And there's no water, and they're burnt so now they have to be carried. Never let your characters get what they want easily, keep it just out of reach. Keep inventing problems for them, some accidental. It's OK for *problems* to be random and accidental, you just can't make the *solutions* random and accidental—your characters have to solve their own problems with wit and effort. If they only have one thing you need them to do, break that action down into twenty individual steps, then throw a wrench in each step. Also, don't make it all environmental. Act Two is also about deepening relationships with your characters, as they get to know each other, and themselves.

Plus, with all the stressful stuff going on, tempers are short, somebody is lying to the MC, the MC is hiding the truth from someone they care about, they are feeling guilty for something, they are (probably) confused by their conflicting feelings towards someone else. Each action scene is usually followed by a short scene of reflection and planning (they make a plan, they succeed or fail, then they make a new plan for the next step). And often you'll want to alternate your scenes emotionally, so you'll have a positive, uplifting or peaceful scene followed by a devastating one.

I've marked the midpoint, but not the pinch points (they'll go roughly in the middle between the midpoints and the first and second plot points).

Map out your scenes for Act Two. List only the location and "what happens."

-
-
-
-
-
-
-
-
-
-

-
-
-
-
-
-
-
-
-
-

Map out your scenes for Act Two. List only the location and "what happens."

-
-
-
-
-
-
-
-
-
-

-
-
-
-
-
-
-
-
-
-

Draw a scene. Draw the central conflict or problem. Symbolize it in a centering object. What can you add to make the scene unique? What can you add to make it epic? What can you add to deepen character? Where is the flash of color? Where are the boundaries?

Draw a scene. Draw the central conflict or problem. Symbolize it in a centering object. What can you add to make the scene unique? What can you add to make it epic? What can you add to deepen character? Where is the flash of color? Where are the boundaries?

Draw a scene. Draw the central conflict or problem. Symbolize it in a centering object. What can you add to make the scene unique? What can you add to make it epic? What can you add to deepen character? Where is the flash of color? Where are the boundaries?

Draw a scene. Draw the central conflict or problem. Symbolize it in a centering object. What can you add to make the scene unique? What can you add to make it epic? What can you add to deepen character? Where is the flash of color? Where are the boundaries?

Draw a scene. Draw the central conflict or problem. Symbolize it in a centering object. What can you add to make the scene unique? What can you add to make it epic? What can you add to deepen character? Where is the flash of color? Where are the boundaries?

Draw a scene. Draw the central conflict or problem. Symbolize it in a centering object. What can you add to make the scene unique? What can you add to make it epic? What can you add to deepen character? Where is the flash of color? Where are the boundaries?

Draw a scene. Draw the central conflict or problem. Symbolize it in a centering object. What can you add to make the scene unique? What can you add to make it epic? What can you add to deepen character? Where is the flash of color? Where are the boundaries?

Draw a scene. Draw the central conflict or problem. Symbolize it in a centering object. What can you add to make the scene unique? What can you add to make it epic? What can you add to deepen character? Where is the flash of color? Where are the boundaries?

Draw a scene. Draw the central conflict or problem. Symbolize it in a centering object. What can you add to make the scene unique? What can you add to make it epic? What can you add to deepen character? Where is the flash of color? Where are the boundaries?

Draw a scene. Draw the central conflict or problem.
Symbolize it in a centering object. What can you add to make the scene unique? What can you add to make it epic? What can you add to deepen character? Where is the flash of color? Where are the boundaries?

MIDPOINT

Draw a scene. Draw the central conflict or problem.
Symbolize it in a centering object. What can you add to make the scene unique? What can you add to make it epic? What can you add to deepen character? Where is the flash of color? Where are the boundaries?

Draw a scene. Draw the central conflict or problem. Symbolize it in a centering object. What can you add to make the scene unique? What can you add to make it epic? What can you add to deepen character? Where is the flash of color? Where are the boundaries?

Draw a scene. Draw the central conflict or problem.
Symbolize it in a centering object. What can you add to make the scene unique? What can you add to make it epic? What can you add to deepen character? Where is the flash of color? Where are the boundaries?

Draw a scene. Draw the central conflict or problem.
Symbolize it in a centering object. What can you add to make the scene unique? What can you add to make it epic? What can you add to deepen character? Where is the flash of color? Where are the boundaries?

Draw a scene. Draw the central conflict or problem.
Symbolize it in a centering object. What can you add to make the scene unique? What can you add to make it epic? What can you add to deepen character? Where is the flash of color? Where are the boundaries?

Draw a scene. Draw the central conflict or problem.
Symbolize it in a centering object. What can you add to make the scene unique? What can you add to make it epic? What can you add to deepen character? Where is the flash of color? Where are the boundaries?

Draw a scene. Draw the central conflict or problem. Symbolize it in a centering object. What can you add to make the scene unique? What can you add to make it epic? What can you add to deepen character? Where is the flash of color? Where are the boundaries?

Draw a scene. Draw the central conflict or problem. Symbolize it in a centering object. What can you add to make the scene unique? What can you add to make it epic? What can you add to deepen character? Where is the flash of color? Where are the boundaries?

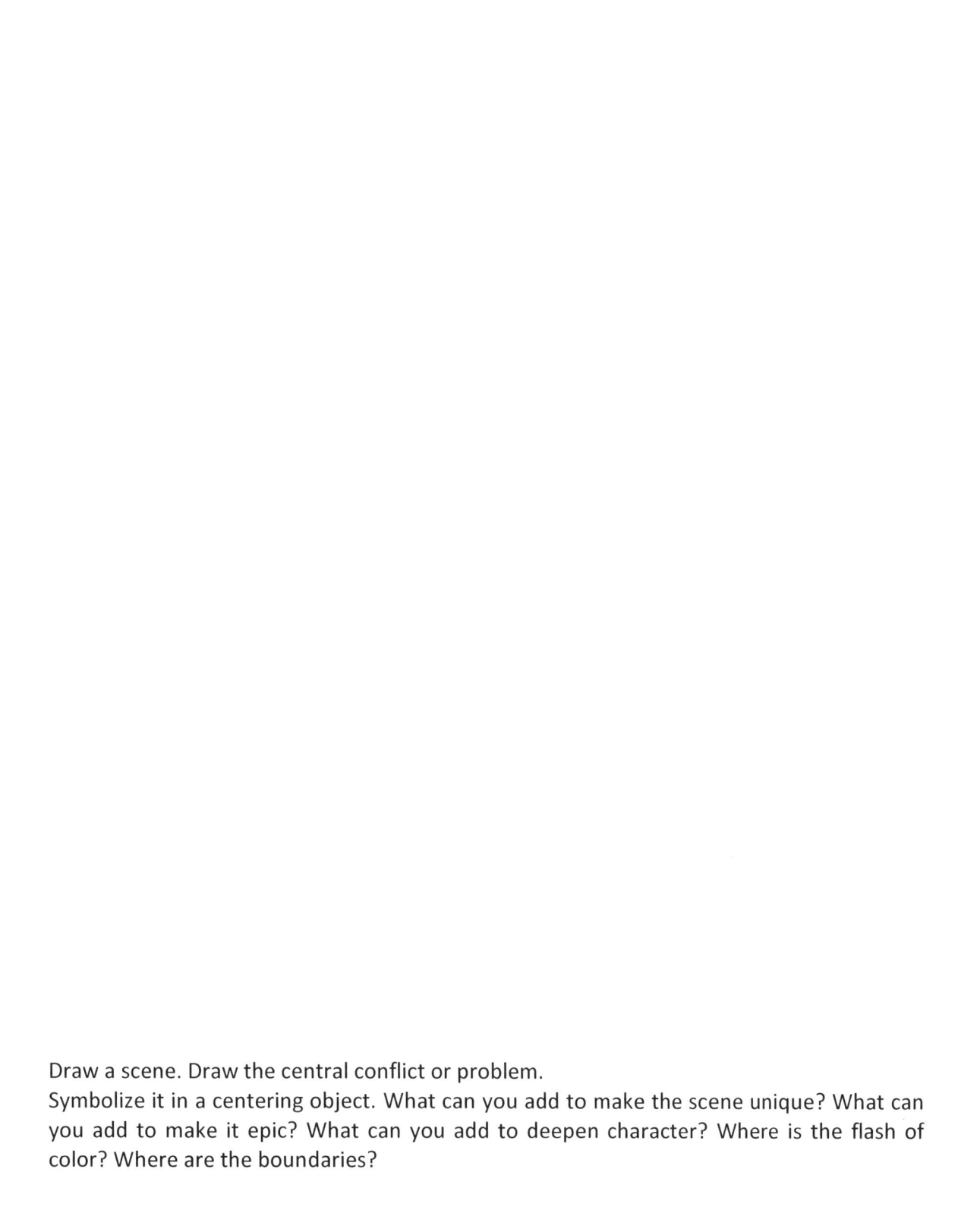

Draw a scene. Draw the central conflict or problem. Symbolize it in a centering object. What can you add to make the scene unique? What can you add to make it epic? What can you add to deepen character? Where is the flash of color? Where are the boundaries?

Draw a scene. Draw the central conflict or problem. Symbolize it in a centering object. What can you add to make the scene unique? What can you add to make it epic? What can you add to deepen character? Where is the flash of color? Where are the boundaries?

Draw a scene. Draw the central conflict or problem. Symbolize it in a centering object. What can you add to make the scene unique? What can you add to make it epic? What can you add to deepen character? Where is the flash of color? Where are the boundaries?

SECOND PLOT POINT

Draw a scene. Draw the central conflict or problem.
Symbolize it in a centering object. What can you add to make the scene unique? What can you add to make it epic? What can you add to deepen character? Where is the flash of color? Where are the boundaries?

Mapping it out
(Act Three)

The Third Act will have about 10 to 20 chapters and make up about 25% of the story. The Third Act will mostly cover the protagonist dealing with their loss or failure, feeling overwhelmed, getting a pep talk or finding a meaningful reason to persevere, formulating a new plan of action, and/or being forced into a final confrontation with the antagonist. They'll succeed, but they'll have to give something up (or at least be willing to). In the process, they are forever changed, and when they return to the ordinary world, everything is the same, but they are different.

Map out your scenes for Act Two. List only the location and "what happens."

-
-
-
-
-
-
-
-
-
-

-
-
-
-
-
-
-
-
-
-

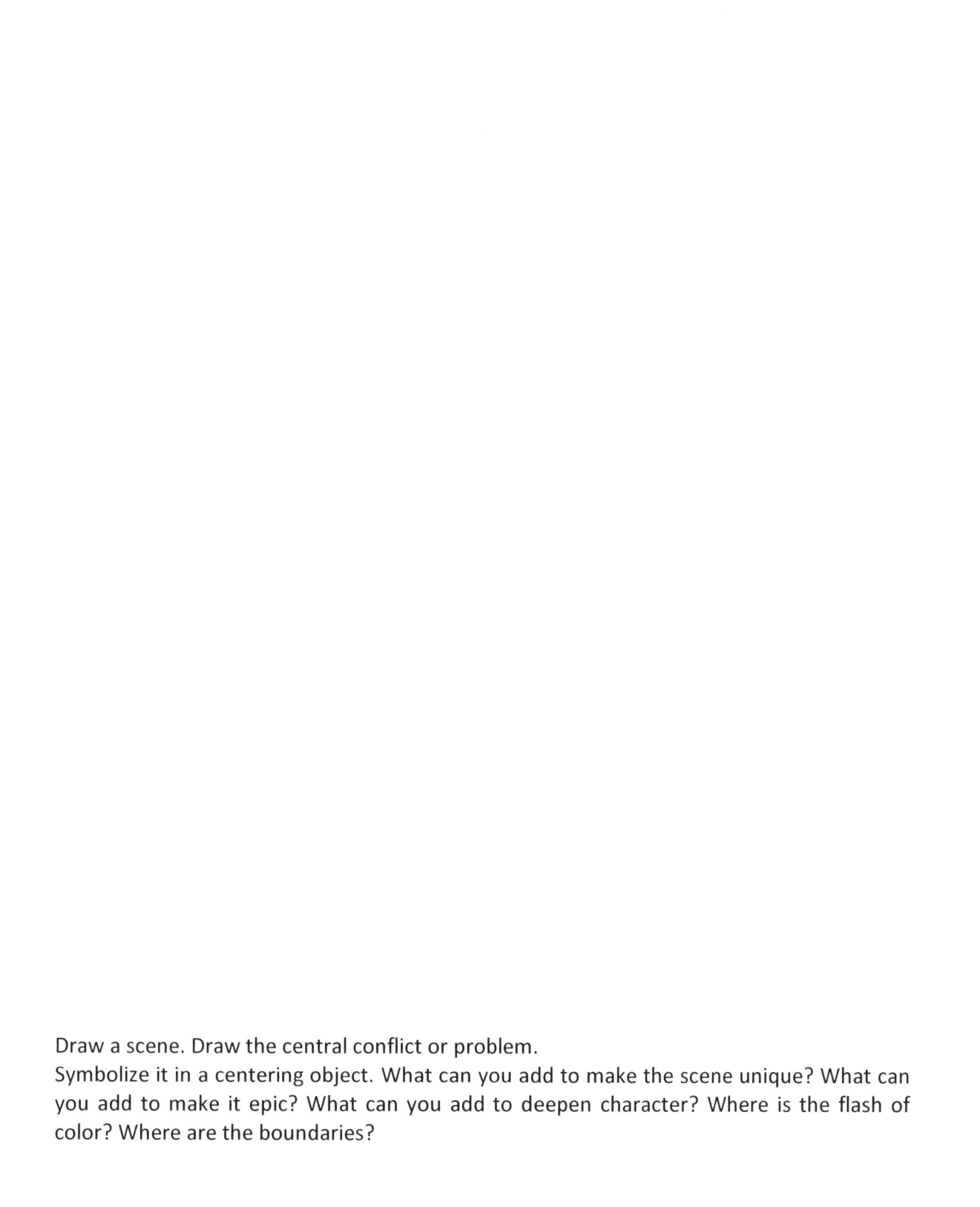

Draw a scene. Draw the central conflict or problem. Symbolize it in a centering object. What can you add to make the scene unique? What can you add to make it epic? What can you add to deepen character? Where is the flash of color? Where are the boundaries?

Draw a scene. Draw the central conflict or problem. Symbolize it in a centering object. What can you add to make the scene unique? What can you add to make it epic? What can you add to deepen character? Where is the flash of color? Where are the boundaries?

Draw a scene. Draw the central conflict or problem.
Symbolize it in a centering object. What can you add to make the scene unique? What can you add to make it epic? What can you add to deepen character? Where is the flash of color? Where are the boundaries?

Draw a scene. Draw the central conflict or problem. Symbolize it in a centering object. What can you add to make the scene unique? What can you add to make it epic? What can you add to deepen character? Where is the flash of color? Where are the boundaries?

Draw a scene. Draw the central conflict or problem.
Symbolize it in a centering object. What can you add to make the scene unique? What can you add to make it epic? What can you add to deepen character? Where is the flash of color? Where are the boundaries?

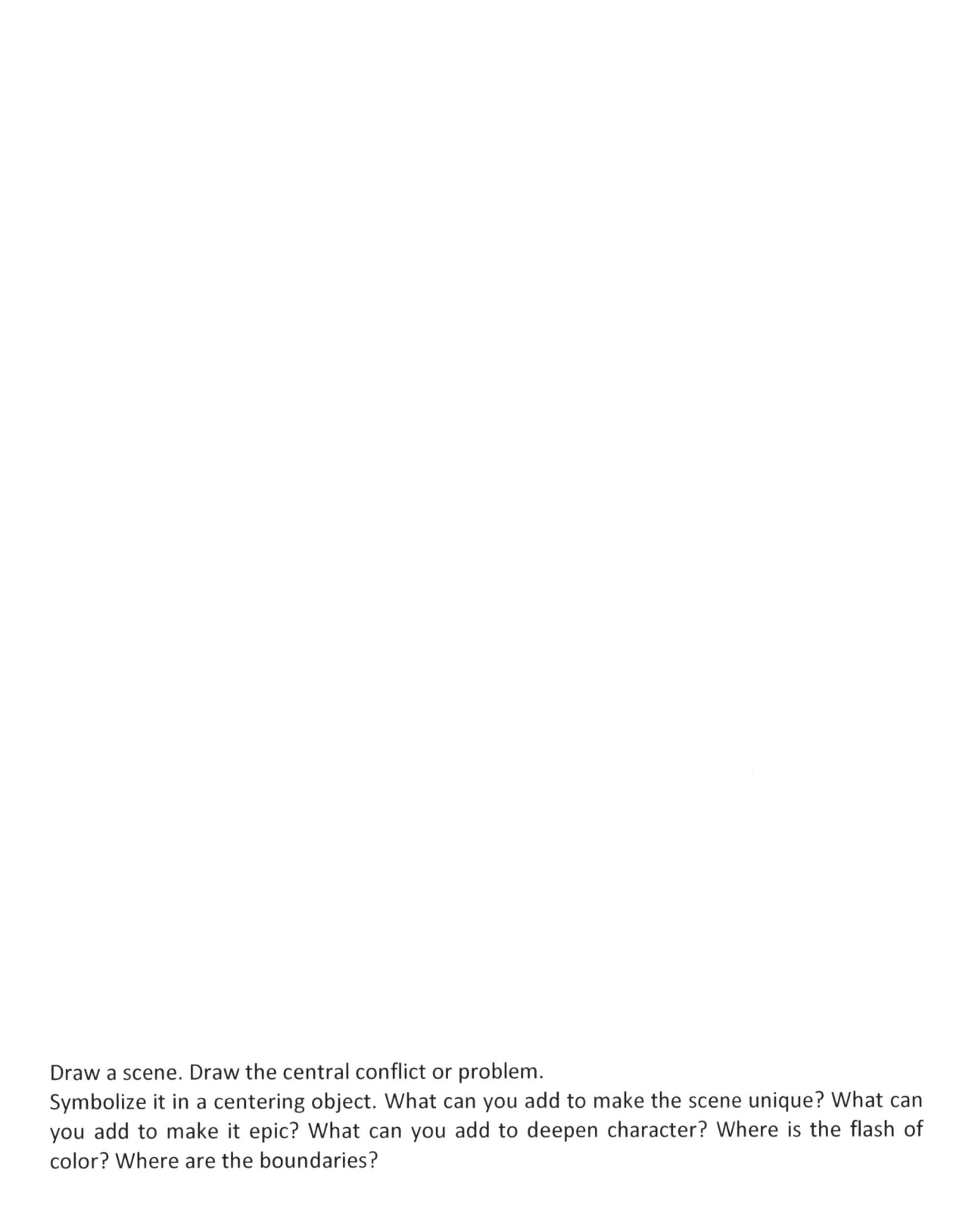

Draw a scene. Draw the central conflict or problem. Symbolize it in a centering object. What can you add to make the scene unique? What can you add to make it epic? What can you add to deepen character? Where is the flash of color? Where are the boundaries?

Draw a scene. Draw the central conflict or problem.
Symbolize it in a centering object. What can you add to make the scene unique? What can you add to make it epic? What can you add to deepen character? Where is the flash of color? Where are the boundaries?

Draw a scene. Draw the central conflict or problem. Symbolize it in a centering object. What can you add to make the scene unique? What can you add to make it epic? What can you add to deepen character? Where is the flash of color? Where are the boundaries?

Draw a scene. Draw the central conflict or problem. Symbolize it in a centering object. What can you add to make the scene unique? What can you add to make it epic? What can you add to deepen character? Where is the flash of color? Where are the boundaries?

Draw a scene. Draw the central conflict or problem. Symbolize it in a centering object. What can you add to make the scene unique? What can you add to make it epic? What can you add to deepen character? Where is the flash of color? Where are the boundaries?

Draw a scene. Draw the central conflict or problem. Symbolize it in a centering object. What can you add to make the scene unique? What can you add to make it epic? What can you add to deepen character? Where is the flash of color? Where are the boundaries?

FINAL BATTLE

Draw your Final Battle Scene again. Make it bigger, bolder. Make the setting distinctive and amazing. Draw the MC faltering, before coming back to triumph. What is the AC hoping for? What does the MC need to learn/accept before their victory?

Draw a final "resolution" scene. Even if you don't have a final chapter or two after the climax, you should draw a picture of what your MC does the day after. How do they feel? How are they treated by others?

The Writing Process

Having a map of your story, and having pictured the scenes in detail, will help with the writing process, but that doesn't mean it will be easy. Here are some final tips to help you *finish* writing your book.

1. Write the rough draft quickly. Don't edit, don't improve the writing, don't focus on the sentences. Just block in the conversation, setting and action in big chunks. If you get stuck, make a note and move on. Focus on hitting a certain word count, or getting through a chapter a day.
2. Keep going until you get to the end. If you get stuck, go back to the beginning and start revising and cleaning things up. Every time you go through, you discover new things about your story and characters.
3. Get to the end. Clean it up enough to send to beta readers (or your mom), but keep focusing on the *story*, not the writing, until you're sure the story is enjoyable and satisfying. At this point, I recommend reading *The Story Grid* by Shawn Coyne and *Story Fix* by Larry Brooks.

4. Then start revising in earnest. Don't get discouraged that the writing may not be that great yet. Those sentences don't start to shine until the last few rounds of editing.
5. Kill your darlings, which means, any sentence you're really proud of because it's such *great writing* probably needs to be cut (readers don't want to be impressed with the writing if it distracts from the story. Stick with the story, use the words that convey the right images and emotions, but don't overdo it.
6. Writing is a learnable skill! You don't really understand what it takes to write a book until you've finished one, and even then, you're just a beginner. Be proud of yourself, but recognize you may need a professional editor, and also to finish several more books (probably both) before you start producing high quality work.
7. That said, "quality" isn't necessarily an indicator of commercial success. If you can't find an agent or publisher, don't be afraid to self-publish and get your work out there. Who knows what could happen.
8. Different genres have different expected lengths, but a normal first novel should be between 60K (young adult) and 90K (epic fantasy). If you're shooting for 60K and 60 chapters, each chapter will be around 1000 words, and shouldn't be over 2000 words—but that's on average. Some will be longer or shorter.

Thanks!

I hope this book helps you. If it does, please share it and post a review. You can also say hi to me online:

Twitter.com/creativindie

Facebook.com/creativindie

PS. If you draw some scenes you're really proud of, please share and tag me – you can use the hashtag #plotdot or #visualplotting.

About the Author

Derek Murphy is working on a PhD in Taiwan, has studied fine art in Italy, and has been living abroad for over a decade. He's spoken at dozens of publishing conferences and events around the world about how to write, design and market books that sell. After founding a successful book editing company and cover design business, he recently resolved to write and publish his own fiction.

Now he has time to focus on his own creative projects, and helps authors and artists do the same through his blog, www.CreativIndie.com

Made in the USA
Charleston, SC
15 April 2016